Turn-to-Learn
MATH
LEARNING WHEELS

20 Ready-to-Reproduce Patterns
That Put a New Spin on Math Skill-Building!

SCHOLASTIC
PROFESSIONAL BOOKS

New York • Toronto • London • Auckland • Sydney

Acknowledgment Page

· · · · · · · · · · · · · · · ·

To my children Rick, Tony, Steve and Betsy. And to all of my students who have enjoyed learning math with math wheels.

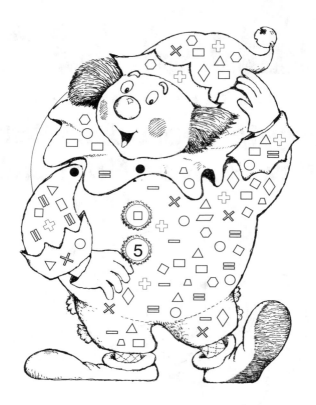

Cover design by Vincent Ceci and Jaime Lucero
Cover and interior illustrations by Bob Alley
Interior design by Robert Dominguez and Jaime Lucero for Grafica

Table of Contents
· · · · · · · · · · · · ·

• • • • • • • • • Welcome to Math Wheels! • • • • • • • •

Math Wheels are a fun-filled interactive alternative to flash cards and worksheets that present math facts in a game format that children love. Because they invite children to take skill-building into their own hands, Math Wheels are a powerful learning tool you and your students will enjoy using again and again. Each engaging shape is designed to complement popular classroom themes. What's more, because the wheels are self-correcting (all students have to do is flip the moving answer-hider to reveal the solution), they offer children instant feedback. And, if a child does miss a problem, a turn of the wheel provides a fresh opportunity to try again. Some of the wheels are interchangeable (Plus, Minus and Times) so if, for example, you are doing a dinosaur unit, you can enhance the unit by pairing the dinosaur shape with the problem wheel that addresses the math skill of your choice.

Math Wheels are perfect for use with the whole class, in small group settings, and for individual one-on-one practice. They can be used as the focus of a teacher-directed activity, or placed in a learning center for children to use independently or in pairs. And best of all, Math Wheels are easy to make and simple to store.

Putting Math Wheels Together

Whenever possible, involve children in making the wheels themselves.

1. To make the wheels you'll need:
- paper
- markers or crayons
- scissors
- brass fasteners
- glue
- oaktag

You can make the wheels in the following ways:
- Simply photocopy the patterns, cut, and color;
- Photocopy the patterns and paste them to oaktag (or manila folders) for added durability, cut and color;
- Photocopy the patterns onto colored paper, paste them to oaktag, and cut them out;
- Photocopy the patterns directly onto oaktag if your copier allows, and cut them out.

2. Next, cut open the windows. While older students may be able to do this on their own, younger ones may need some help. In either case it helps to use small pointed scissors.

3. Once you've created the character, use a brass fastener to attach the problem wheel through the ✖ checking to be sure that the problems and the answers appear in the windows. Use a second brass fastener to attach the moveable answer-hider through the circle ⊕.

● ● ● ● ● ● ● ● ● ● ● ● ● **CONSTRUCTION TIPS** ● ● ● ● ● ● ● ● ● ● ● ● ●

1. Color contrasts: You can copy each problem wheel onto colored paper that contrasts with the color of the character. This contrast makes it easier for children to focus on the information that appears in the character's windows.

2. Laminated wheels: If you would like to make sturdier wheels, try laminating them.

3. Textured wheels: You can give your Math Wheels added texture by covering them with colored felt or yarn, cotton balls, or glitter. You can also add googlie eyes.

4. Oversized wheels: While students will love having their own Math Wheels, you may want to make an enlarged version to display in a learning center or to use while working with the whole class. To make these oversized versions, simply enlarge the patterns on your copy machine and follow the assembly steps outlined above.

Introducing Math Wheels

Math Wheels are a wonderful tool for practicing or reinforcing math facts. Prior to using the Math Wheels in your class, children may need many opportunities to come to an understanding of the concepts that lie beneath the skills and facts. Concrete activities using manipulatives, coupled with real-life math experiences (measuring, counting, sorting, graphing, estimating, etc.), provide children with the rich background they will need to get the most from Math Wheels.

It is best to introduce the wheels in a small group setting. After demonstrating how to use each wheel, call attention to the operation or skill it features. Show children how one part of each character can be used to hide the answer so they can check their work. Be certain to allow each child a chance to use the wheel with you.

Personifying Math Wheel Characters

Math Wheels come to life when they are treated as class mascots who live in your math corner. Begin by talking to a Math Wheel character as you would talk to a puppet. Here are some simple scenarios to try:

● Pretend that your Math Wheel character doesn't understand the very skill he or she is displaying. Ask children to explain in their own words how to do the math.

TIPS FOR SENSITIVE EVALUATIONS WITH MATH WHEELS

● Children are often sensitive to their own progress without adult intervention or formal yardsticks. Encourage children to play down their competitive spirit and to respond positively to each other's progress as they use the math wheels.

● You might keep some manipulatives—connecting cubes or counters—on hand. Then, as you work through problems with the Math Wheels, invite children to use the manipulatives to demonstrate how they arrived at each answer.

● Notice if any children are repeatedly stumped by particular problems or skills. It's possible that these children need additional concrete experiences in order to understand the underlying math concepts.

- Have Math Wheel characters await your children at the classroom door. Invite students to solve a Math Wheel problem as they enter the room or leave for recess.

- When you have a few moments to spare (lining up to go somewhere, waiting for dismissal, etc.) use your character to dialogue with children about the math they learned that day.

Customizing Math Wheels

You and your students can create your own Math Wheel characters like the baseball wheel shown here using the blank problem wheel templates on page 47. Once you've created the characters and are ready to attach the problem wheel, check to be sure that the problems and answers show through the windows properly.

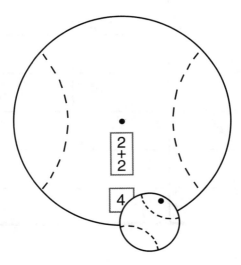

More Math Wheel Ideas

● String a length of clothesline or yarn across a bulletin board; hang the line low enough so children can reach it. Place each character and one or more of the problem wheels you've already introduced to the group into a self-closing plastic bag. Use a paint marker (available from art supply stores) to label each bag. Use a clothespin to clip each bag to the line and invite children to access them throughout the day.

● Create a Math Wheel display to enliven the classroom and to help you keep track of which wheels each student has used. Cover a bulletin board with colorful paper. Tack the Math Wheels across the top of the display. Use a marker to draw vertical lines between the wheels and then draw horizontal lines across the board creating enough boxes under each Math Wheel for your students. Write their names to the left of the chart. As students are introduced to a particular Math Wheel, invite them to place an X or a sticker in the box below the character that corresponds with their name.

This will help you and your students keep track of the work they are doing.

Students				
Jaime				
Ingrid				
Robert				
Liza				
Tony				
Carmen				

● You can use completed wheels to make a class book of math story problems. Have students pick their favorite characters to include. Review some of the common language used in story problems—how many altogether? How many left? Then, have each student write a story problem about the character of their choice using the math skill it addresses. Students should write and illustrate their problem on one page and paste their math wheel to the opposite page. Children will enjoy presenting their story problems and solving their classmates'.

Home School Connection

● Math Wheels are a perfect addition to a take-home thematic backpack program. Be certain to include a letter explaining the importance of using Math Wheels with children, copies of blank problem wheels (page 47) for families to customize, as well as some tips for use at home. Don't forget to invite family feedback! We've included a sample letter you may adapt to fit your own needs on page 10.

● You might even ask parents to volunteer to make Math Wheels at home. Working parents who find it almost impossible to volunteer during the school day may welcome this chance to help out—and children will beam with pride when characters created in their homes are used in class.

Dear Families,

It's your child's turn to bring home one of our Math Wheels! In class we use these Math Wheels to help strengthen and reinforce the math facts we have learned. Your child can show you how these wheels work. Try holding and turning the wheel as your child answers the problems featured there. Then, work with your child to make up some new problems of your own using the blank wheel included here. Let your child lead the way and you should have a great time practicing math facts together.

Thank you for your participation.

Sincerely,

_____
Your Child's Teacher

The Wheels

· · · · · · · · · · · · ·

Counting Bear

Here's a bear you can count on to strengthen counting skills again and again!

• • • • • • • • • **EXTENDING THE LEARNING** • • • • • • • • • •

Ask students to turn their wheels so that the lowest number appears in the window. Invite children to add numbers (Add 2; add 3; add 1, etc. . .) totaling any number up to 10. Children should turn their wheels to keep a running count. When the series of directions is complete, check to see if each child has arrived at the same number.

COUNTING BEAR
Pattern

Cut
out

Cut
out

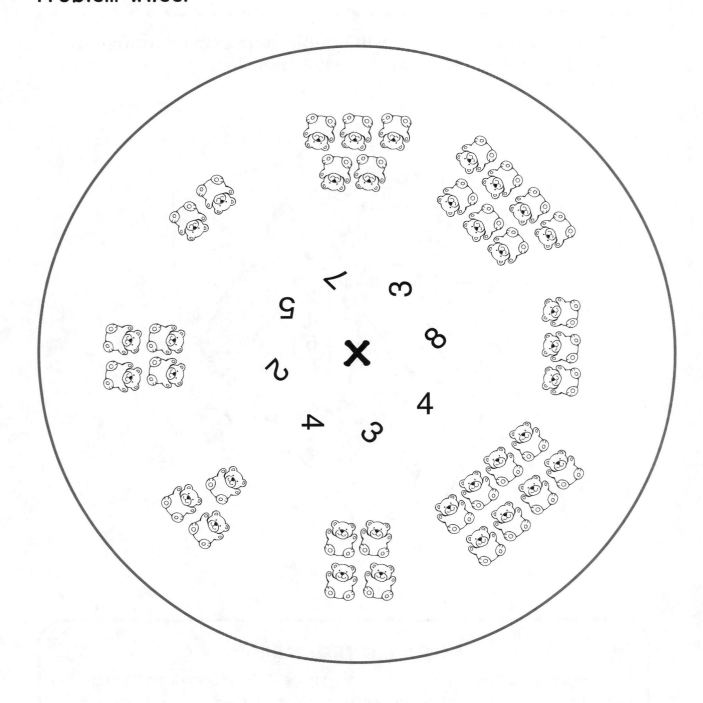

Two-ie the Toucan

You bet your beak this bird will double your skip counting fun!
You might want to give Two-ie a whole new look by pasting on
colorful feathers.

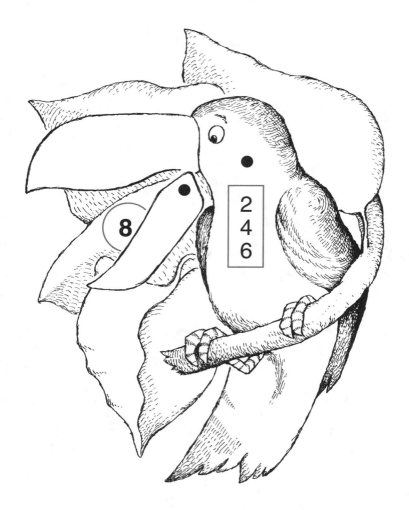

TWO-IE THE TOUCAN
● ● ● ● ● ● ● ● ● ● ● ● ● ● ●
Pattern

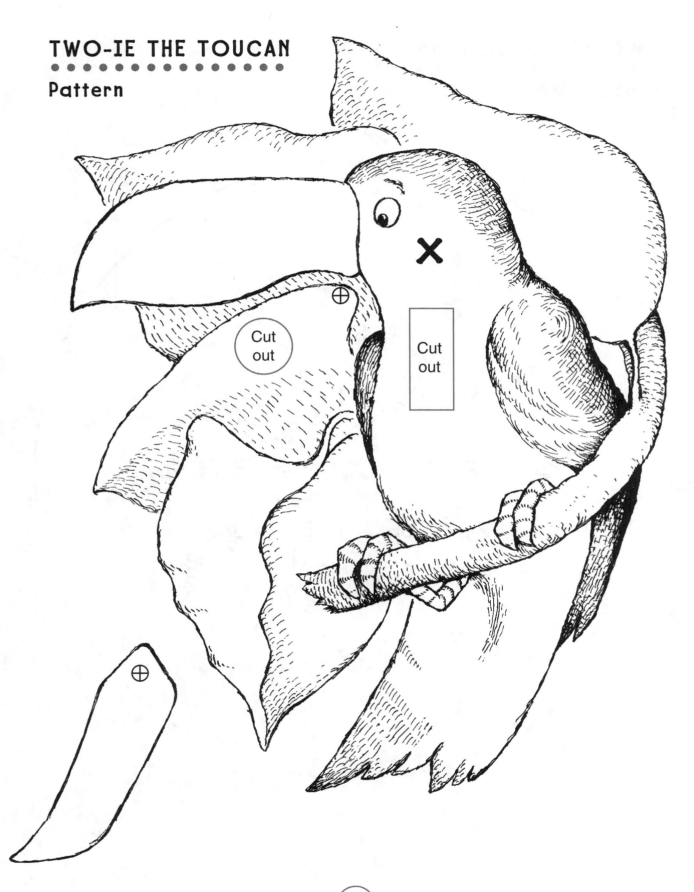

TWO-IE THE TOUCAN
Problem Wheel

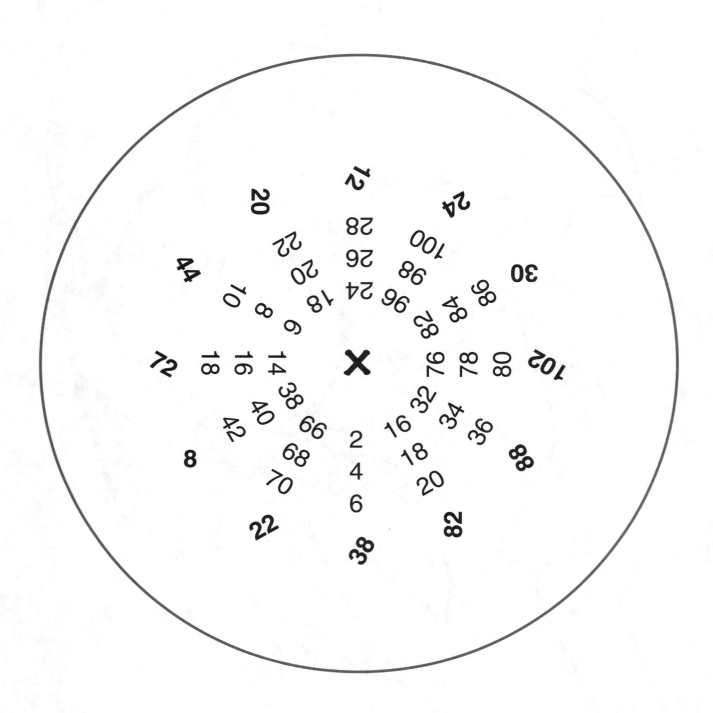

Plus the Cat

This kitty cat provides the *purr*fect way to learn addition family facts!

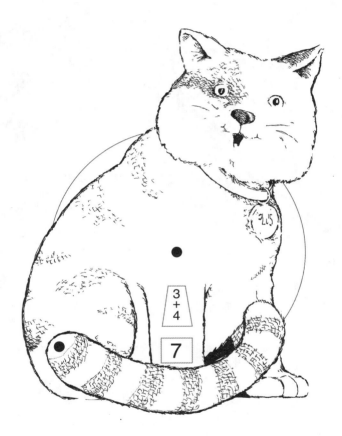

PLUS THE CAT

● ● ● ● ● ● ● ● ●

Pattern

PLUS THE CAT
Problem Wheels

0-5

5-10

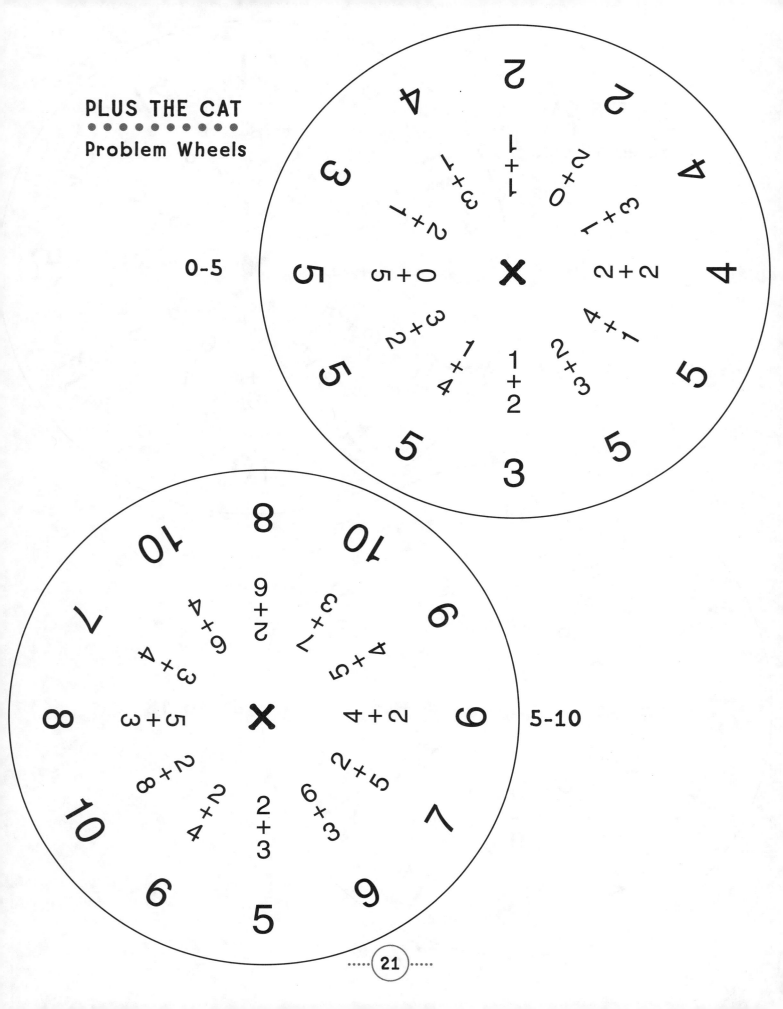

PLUS THE CAT
●●●●●●●●●●●
Problem Wheels

10-15

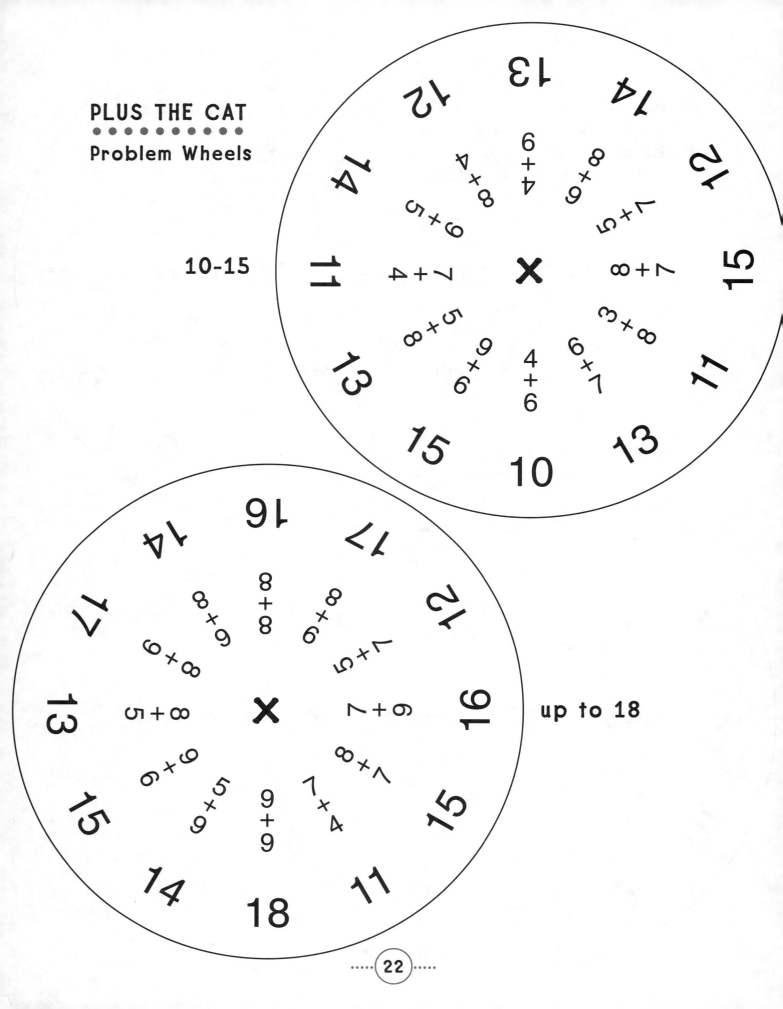

up to 18

Minus the Dog

Take this subtraction pooch for a walk and your students' math skills will really add up!

● ● ● ● ● ● ● ● ● ● **EXTENDING THE LEARNING** ● ● ● ● ● ● ● ● ● ●

Invite students to write stories describing how minus the take-away dog
got his name.

MINUS THE DOG

Pattern

X

Cut out

Cut out

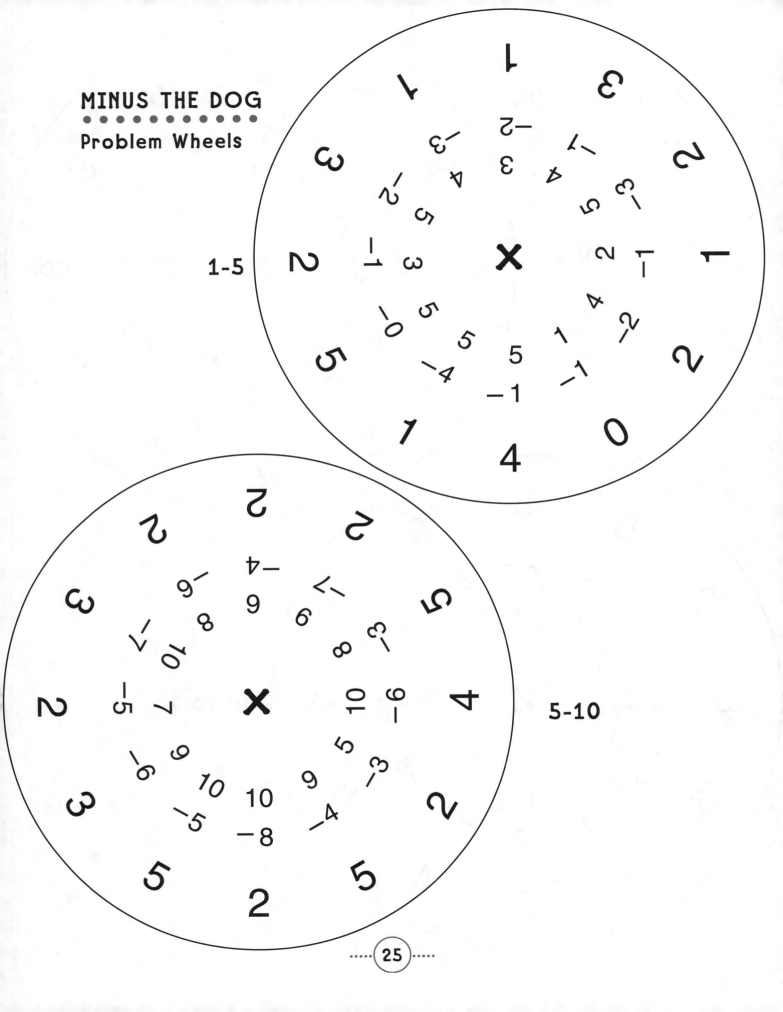

MINUS THE DOG

Problem Wheels

1-5

5-10

MINUS THE DOG

Problem Wheels

10-15

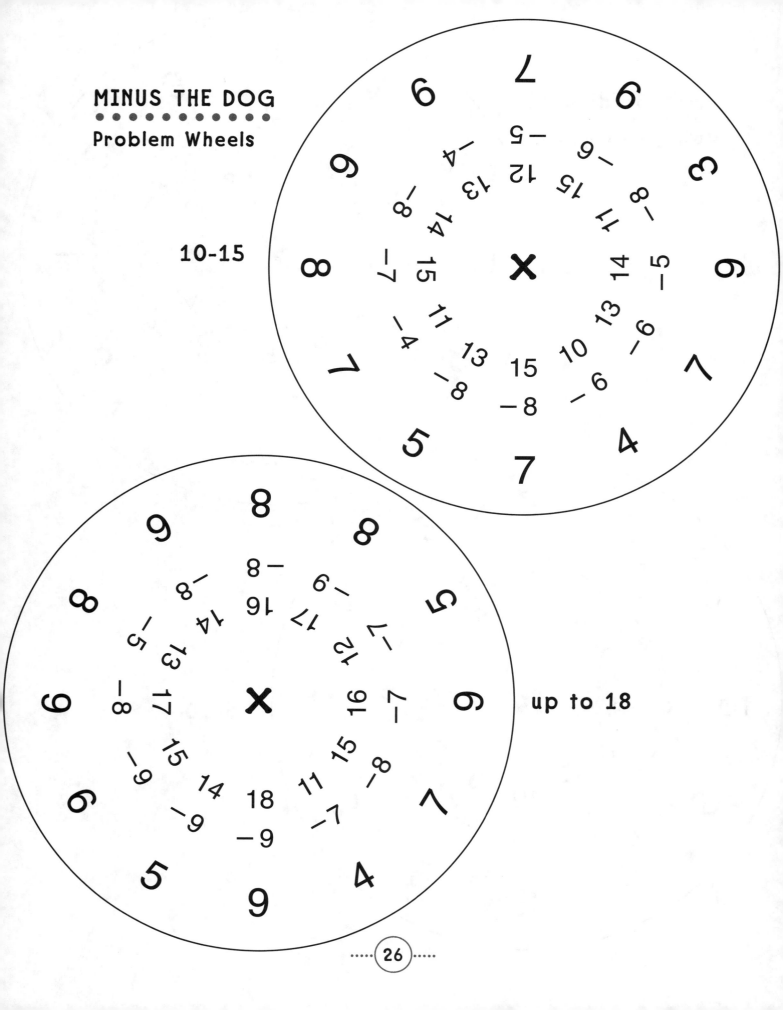

up to 18

Penny the Pig

Penny is a priceless addition to any money unit.

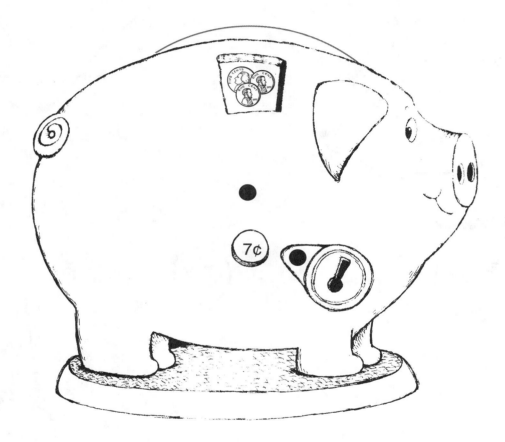

•••••••••• **EXTENDING THE LEARNING** •••••••••••
After children have arrived at the correct sum for each answer, offer them an array of coins and challenge them to arrive at the same sum using as many different coin combinations as they can.

PENNY THE PIG
Pattern

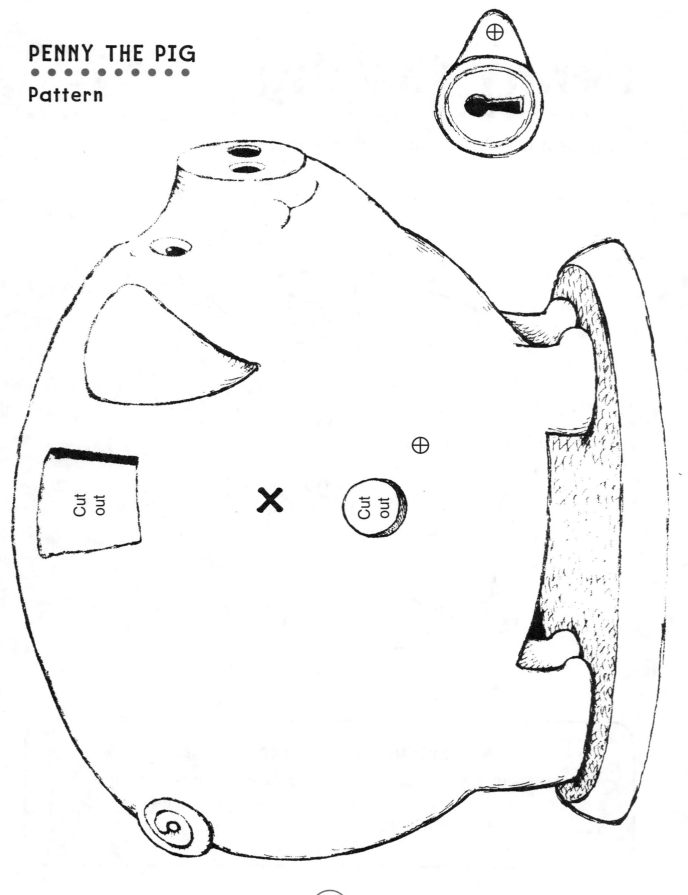

Cut out

Cut out

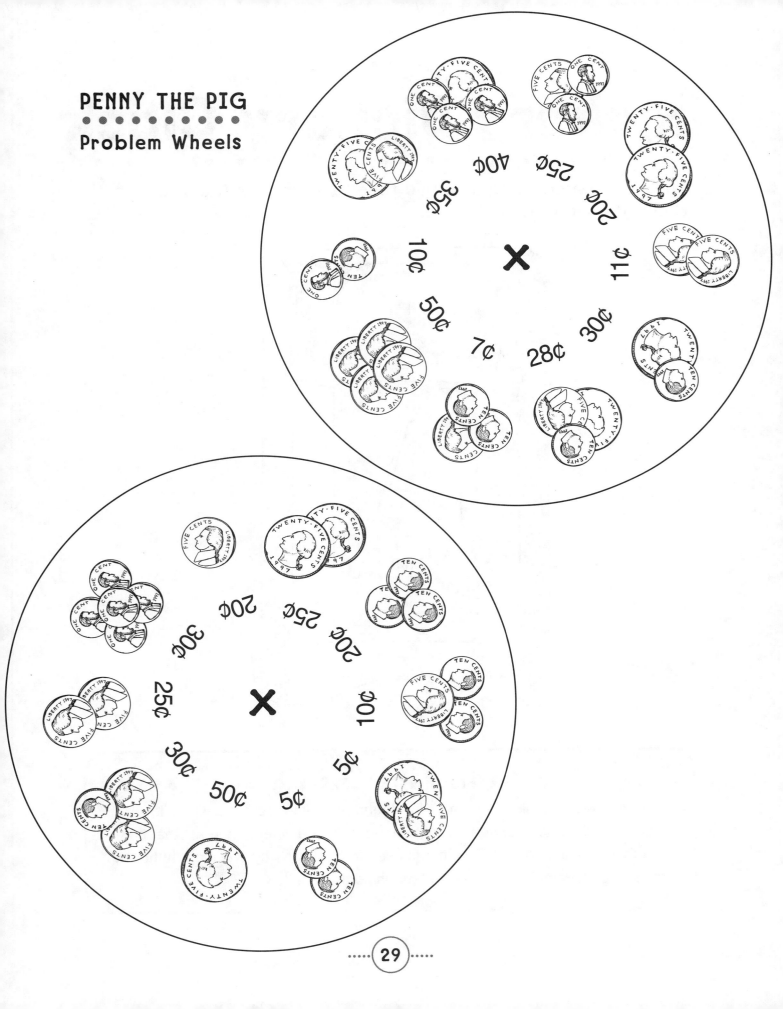

PENNY THE PIG
● ● ● ● ● ● ● ● ●
Problem Wheels

Hickory Dickory Clock

There's no such thing as a bad time to learn how to tell time with Hickory Dickory Clock.

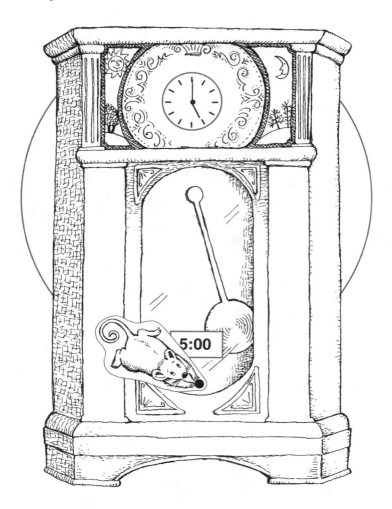

•••••••••• **EXTENDING THE LEARNING** ••••••••••

Ask students to think about how they spend their time. Turn the wheel to reveal a time of your choice. Invite children to share what they do at that time whether it be a.m. or p.m. You might even take the activity one step further by recording students' responses and graphing the results.

HICKORY DICKORY CLOCK

Pattern

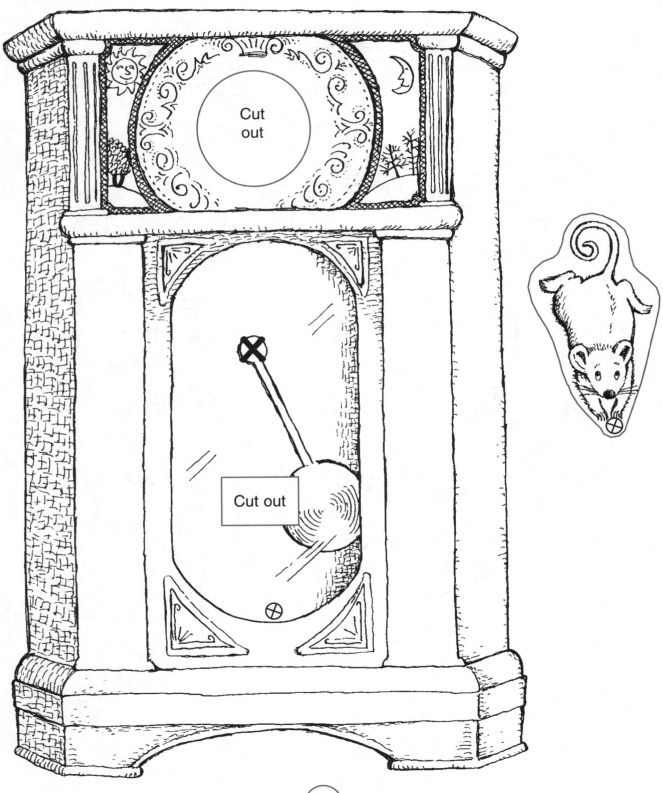

Cut out

Cut out

Hour and Half Hour Wheel

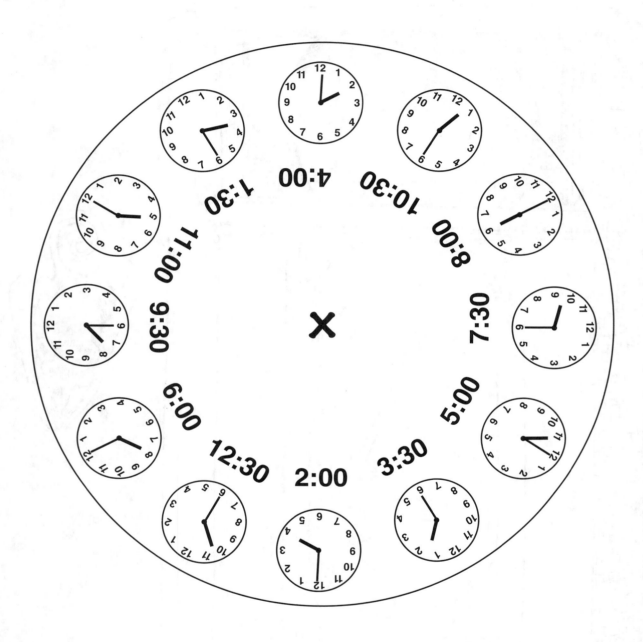

HICKORY DICKORY CLOCK

5 Minute Intervals Wheel

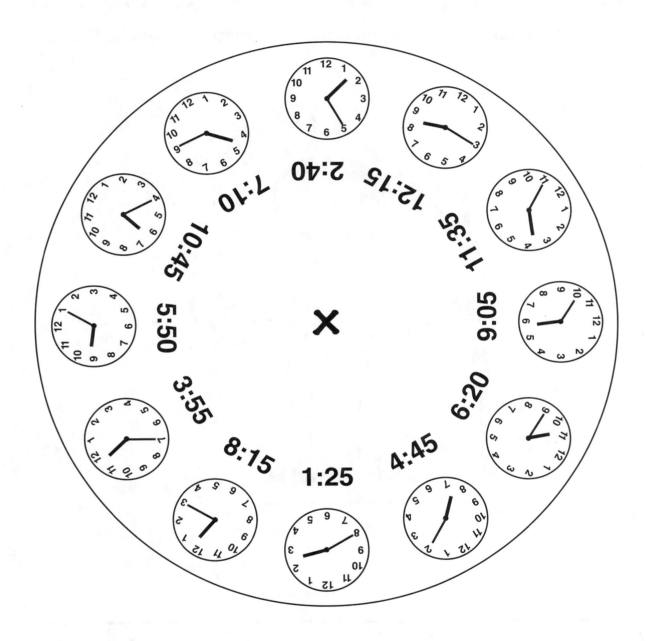

George the Giraffe

Patterning skills won't be such a stretch when George the Giraffe comes to play.

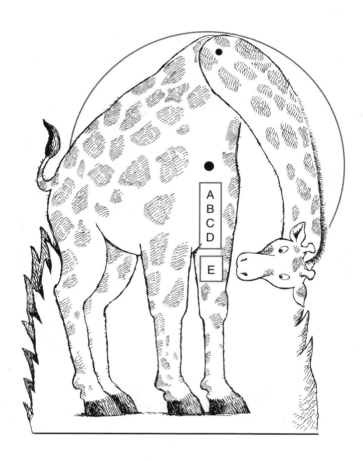

GEORGE THE GIRAFFE

Pattern

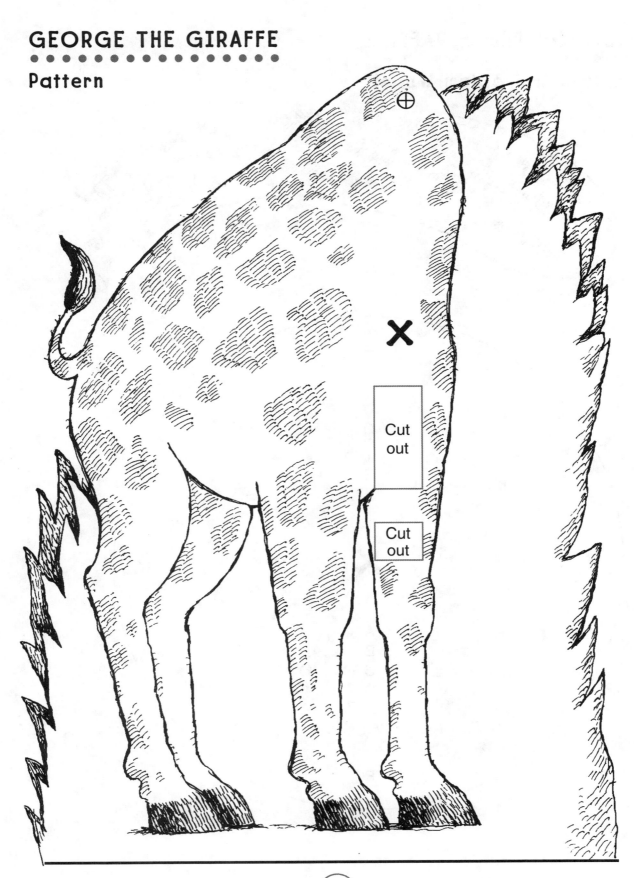

Cut
out

Cut
out

GEORGE THE GIRAFFE
Pattern & Problem Wheel

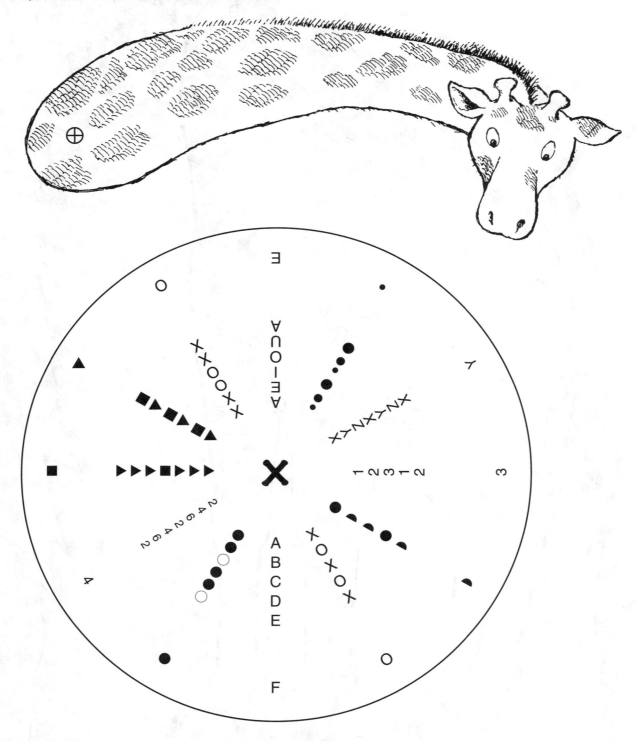

Sam the Shape Clown

Identifying geometric shapes and operation symbols is simple when Sam shows you how.

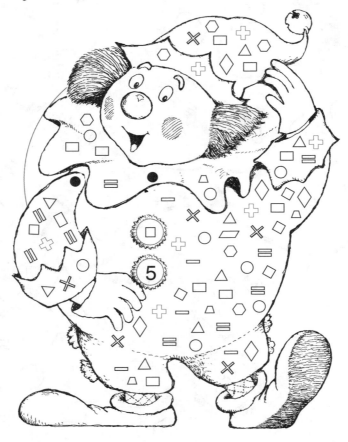

Note: Some students may find it easier to locate and count the shapes and symbols presented here if they are color-coded. While some students may choose to create their own codes, you can suggest they color the images in the following way: square–orange; triangle–green; hexagon–yellow; trapezoid–red; rhombus–blue; parallelogram–tan; circle–pink; rectangle–gray; plus–brown; minus–black; times–purple; equals–light blue.

• • • • • • • • • EXTENDING THE LEARNING • • • • • • • • •

Have children look around the classroom to locate the shapes that appear in Sam's shape window. Ask them to think of other places they see these shapes—on the street, in the store, or in their homes.

SAM THE SHAPE CLOWN
Pattern

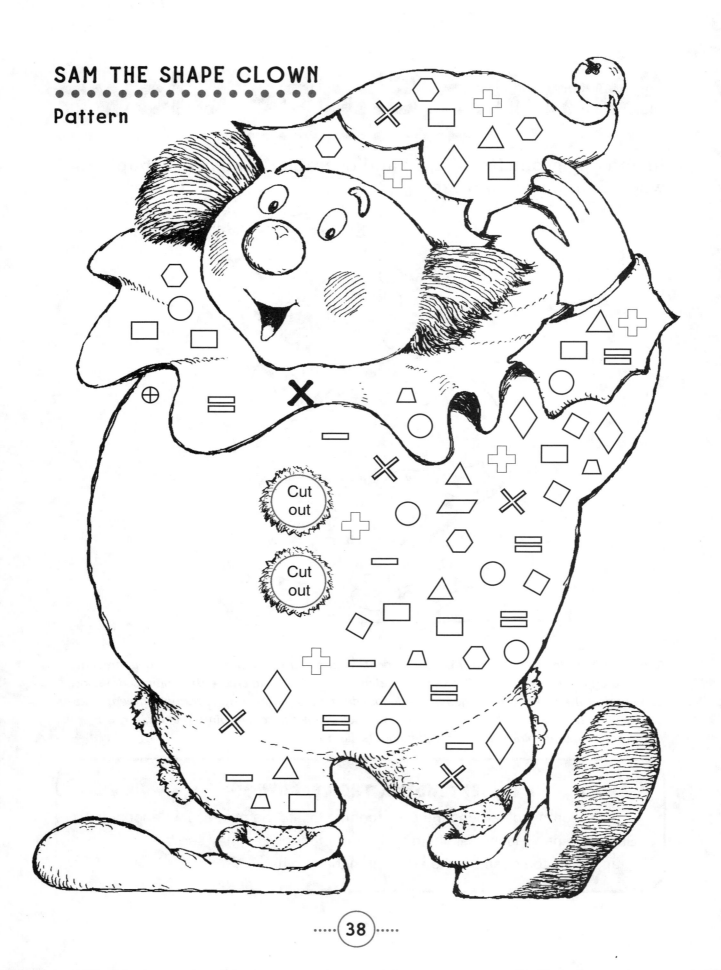

SAM THE SHAPE CLOWN
Pattern & Problem Wheel

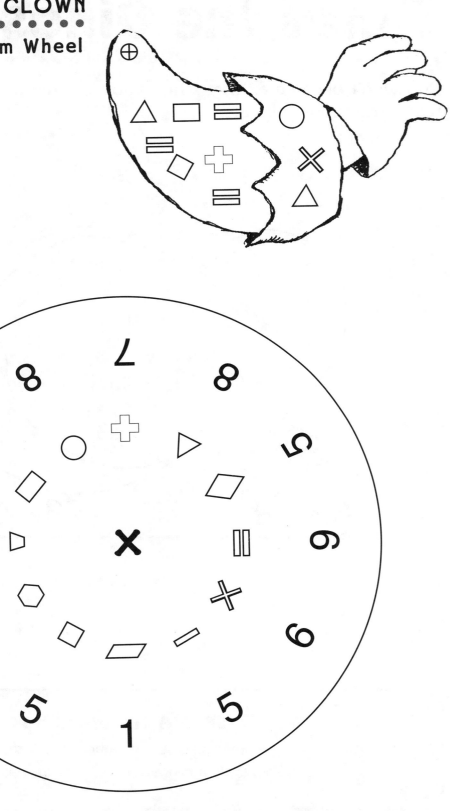

Times the Dinosaur

Fun won't become extinct when you use this friendly dino to teach the times tables!

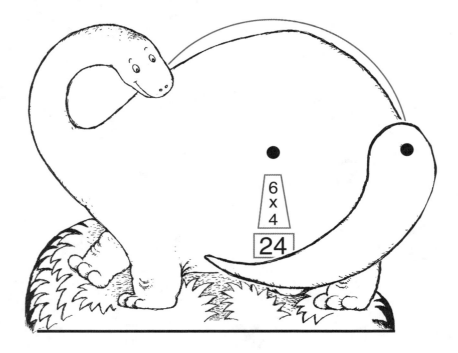

TIMES THE DINOSAUR

Pattern

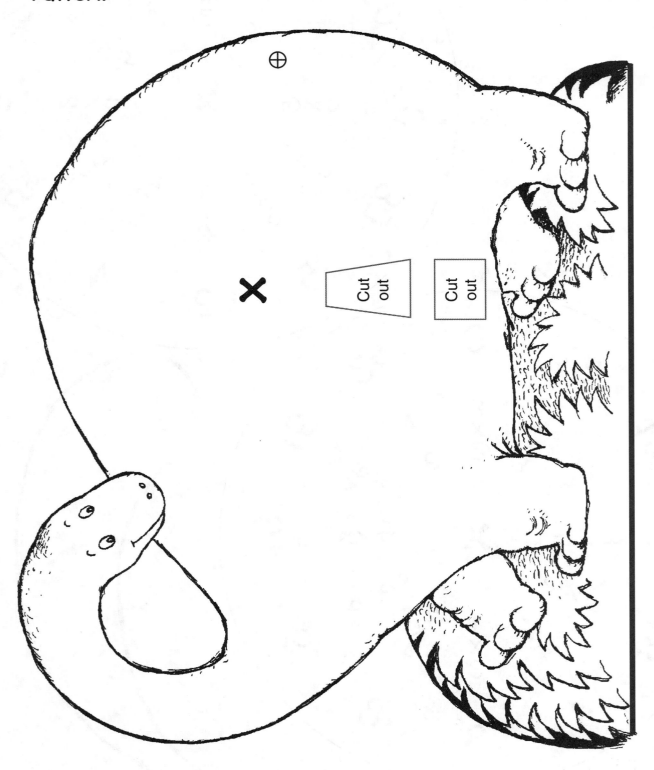

TIMES THE DINOSAUR
• • • • • • • • • • • • • • •
Problem Wheels

2s & 5s

3s & 4s

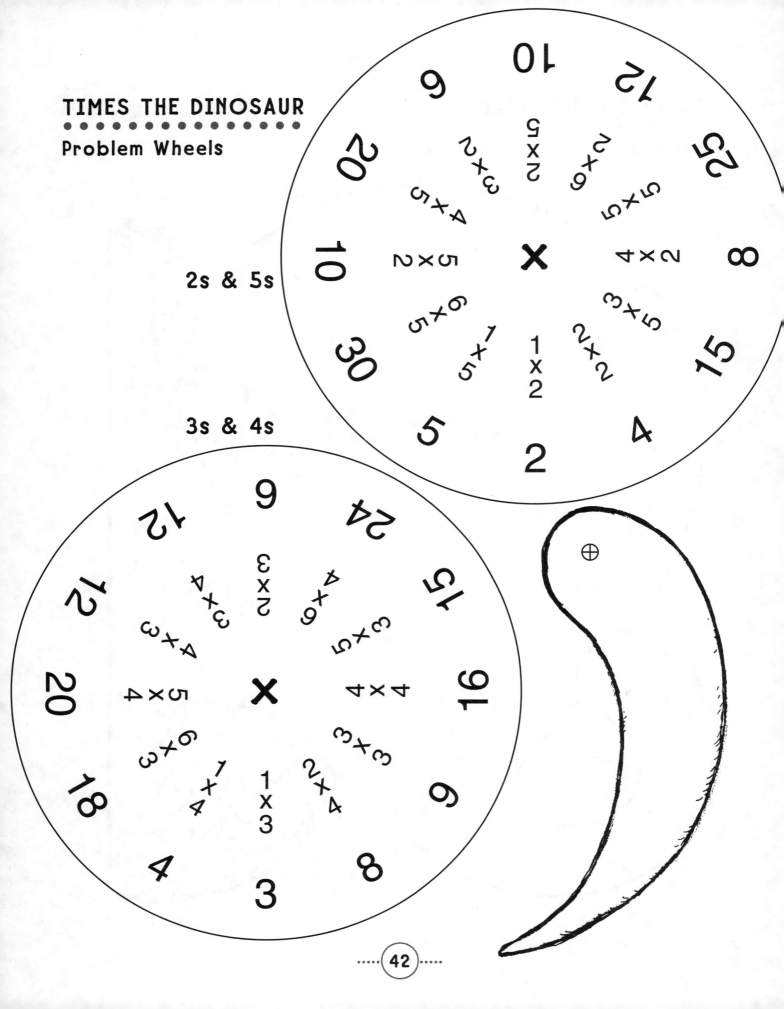

Piece-O-Pizza

You and your students can help yourselves to a tasty slice of fractions!

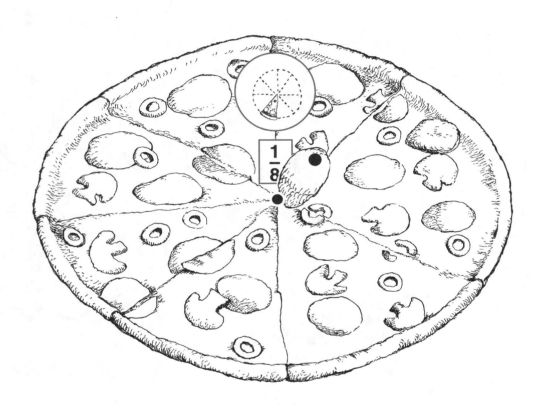

$$\frac{1}{8}$$

PIECE-O-PIZZA
●●●●●●●●●●
Pattern

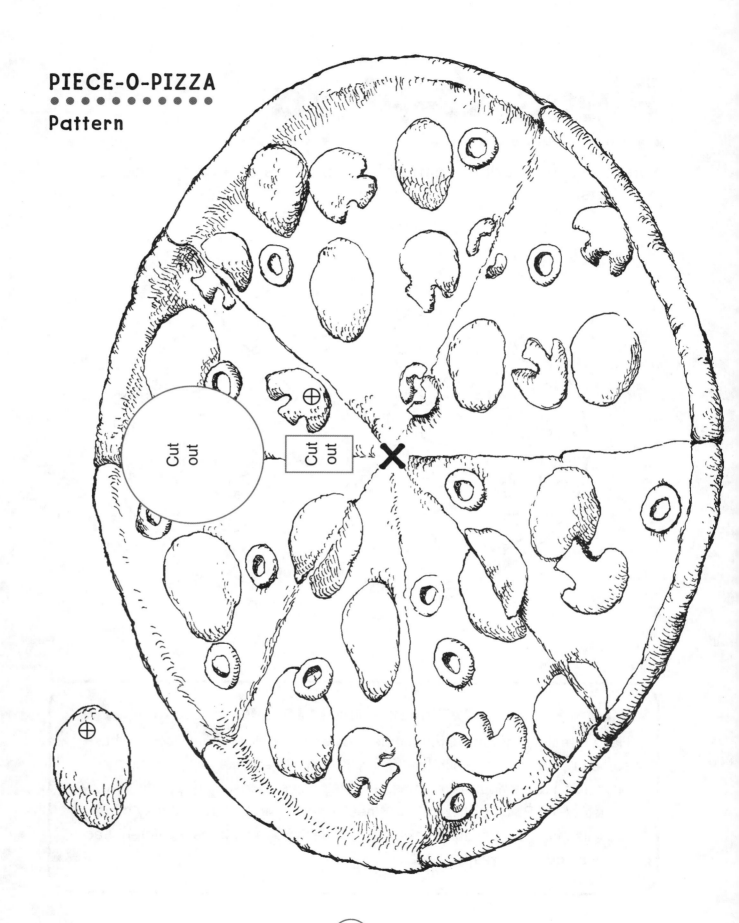

PIECE-O-PIZZA
Problem Wheel
Fraction Remaining

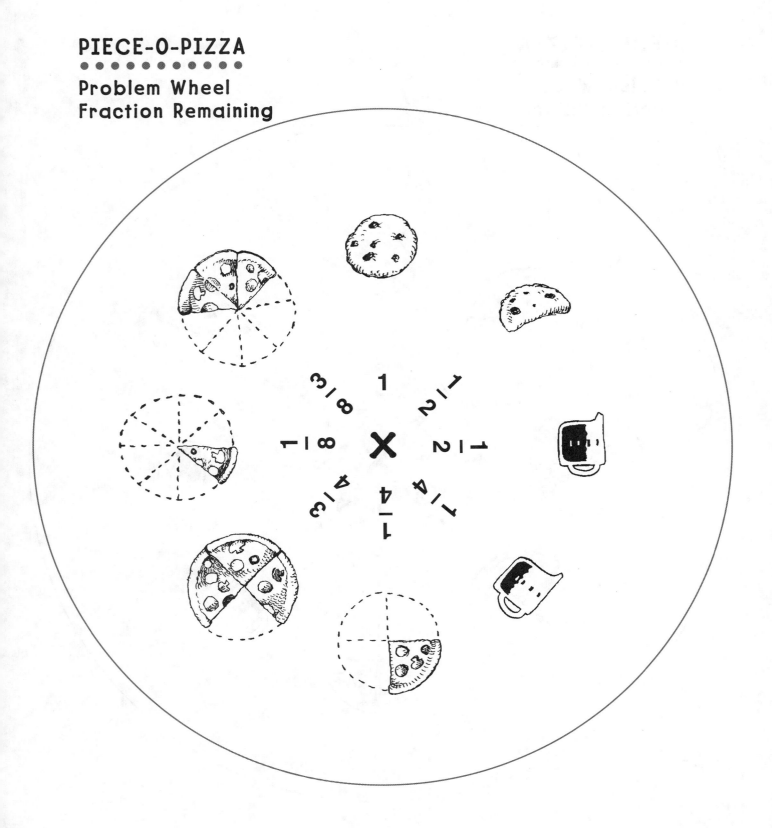

PIECE-O-PIZZA
● ● ● ● ● ● ● ● ● ●
Problem Wheel
Fraction Missing

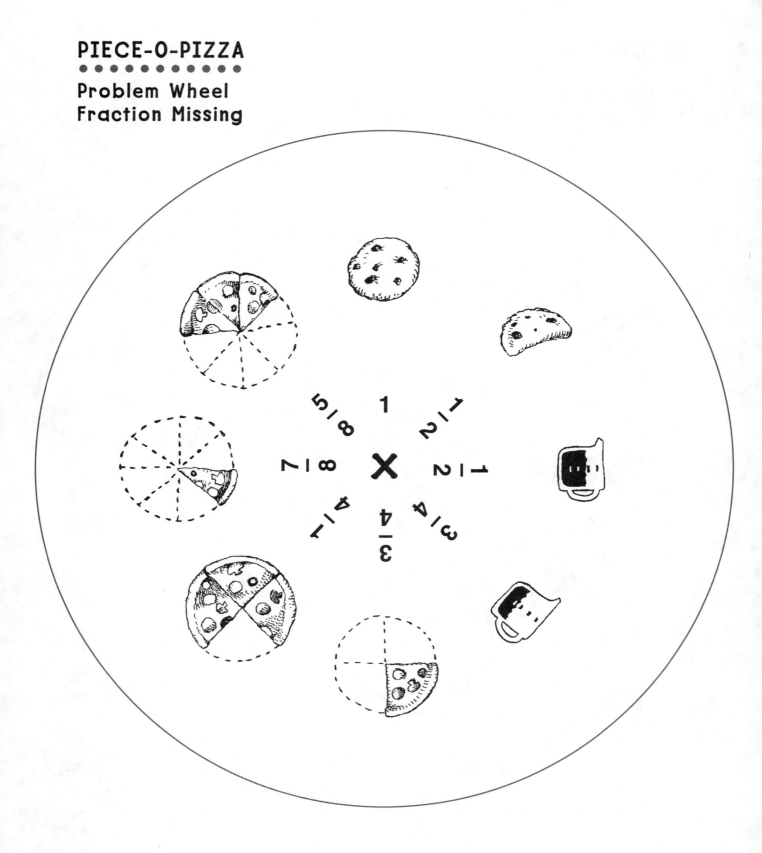

BLANK WHEELS

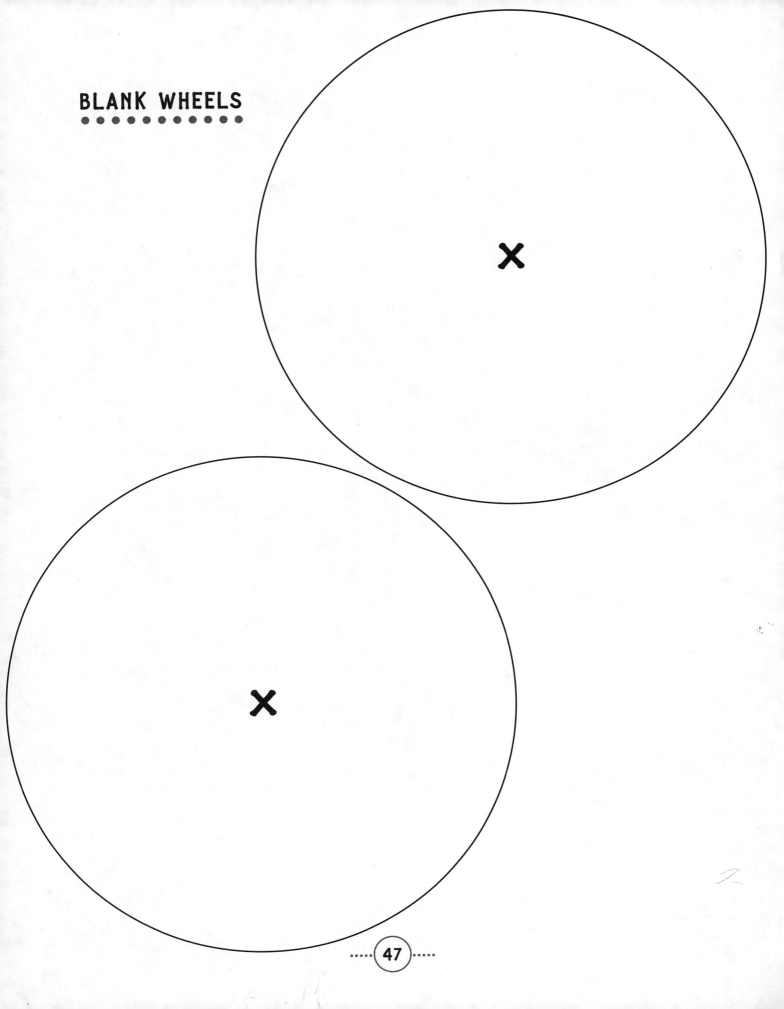

NOTES

●●●●●